Pebble® Plus

Science Builders

Electricity All Around

by Barbara Alpert

Consulting Editor: Gail Saunders-Smith, PhD

Consultant: Joanne K. Olson, PhD
Associate Professor, Science Education
Center for Excellence in Science & Mathematics Education
Iowa State University, Ames

CAPSTONE PRESS
a capstone imprint

Pebble Plus is published by Capstone Press,
151 Good Counsel Drive, P.O. Box 669, Mankato, Minnesota 56002.
www.capstonepub.com

Books published by Capstone Press are manufactured with paper
containing at least 10 percent post-consumer waste.

Library of Congress Cataloging-in-Publication Data
Alpert, Barbara.
  Electricity all around / by Barbara Alpert.
    p. cm.—(Science builders)
  Includes bibliographical references and index.
  Summary: "Simple text and full-color photographs provide a brief introduction to electricity"—Provided by publisher.
  ISBN 978-1-4296-6070-9 (library binding)
  ISBN 978-1-4296-7107-1 (paperback)
  1. Electric wiring—Juvenile literature. 2. Electricity—Juvenile literature. I. Title.
  TK148.A47 2012
  621.3—dc22
                                                                          2010053934

Editorial Credits
Erika L. Shores, editor; Bobbie Nuytten, designer; Wanda Winch, media researcher;
    Laura Manthe, production specialist

Photo Credits
Capstone Studio: Karon Dubke, 9, 19; iStockphoto Inc: Krzysztof Slusarczyk, 17, 22-23, 24; Shutterstock: Arogant, 11,
Christopher Edwin Nuzzaco, 7, Jason Vinz, cover, leungchopan, 1, 21, manfredxy, 15, Natalie Erhove (summerky), 5,
T. W. van Urk, 13

Note to Parents and Teachers

The Science Builders series supports national science standards related to physical science. This
book describes and illustrates electricity. The images support early readers in understanding
the text. The repetition of words and phrases helps early readers learn new words. This book
also introduces early readers to subject-specific vocabulary words, which are defined in the
Glossary section. Early readers may need assistance to read some words and to use the Table of
Contents, Glossary, Read More, Internet Sites, and Index sections of the book.

Printed in the United States of America in North Mankato, Minnesota.
032011   006110CGF11

Table of Contents

What Is Electricity?

What makes holiday lights twinkle?

What makes a fan whir? Electricity!

Electricity is a kind of energy

that makes things work.

Tiny particles called electrons carry energy. The moving electrons provide the energy needed to light lamps and run motors.

Most electricity flows through wires.
Wires are called conductors because
they help electricity get from one
place to another. If you can plug
it in, a machine uses electricity.

Where Electricity Comes From

Power plants make electricity

by burning coal, gas, and oil.

Wires bring electricity from

power plants to homes

and buildings.

Wind and moving water can make electricity too. Wind turns wind turbine blades. Water flows over a dam. Both run machines that make electricity.

13

People also use the sun's power.
Solar panels collect energy
from the sun and turn it
into electricity.

How Electricity Works

Flipping a switch turns on a light. The switch connects wires in a loop called a circuit. Electricity flows in a circuit from power plants to wires inside buildings.

Toys and games often run on electricity from batteries. Batteries store electricity until you need it.

People everywhere need more and more electricity each day. Scientists keep looking for new ways to make electricity.

Glossary

circuit—a path for electricity to flow through

coal—a black or dark brown rock that can burn

conductor—a material that lets electricity travel easily through it

electron—one of the tiny particles that make up all things; protons and neutrons also make up all things

energy—the ability to do work, such as moving things or giving heat or light

oil—a raw material that is found under the ground and turned into a variety of chemicals including gasoline, kerosene, and natural gas

power plant—a building or a group of buildings used to create electricity

wind turbine—an engine that is driven by propellers and uses energy from the wind to make electricity

Read More

Ballard, Carol. *Exploring Electricity.* How Does Science Work? New York: PowerKids Press, 2008.

Boothroyd, Jennifer. *All Charged Up: A Look at Electricity.* Exploring Physical Science. Minneapolis: Lerner Publications, 2011.

Higgins, Nadia *Electricity Is Everywhere.* Science Rocks. Edina, Minn.: Magic Wagon, 2009.

Internet Sites

FactHound offers a safe, fun way to find Internet sites related to this book. All of the sites on FactHound have been researched by our staff.

Here's all you do:

Visit *www.facthound.com*

Type in this code: 9781429660709

Super-cool stuff! Check out projects, games and lots more at www.capstonekids.com

Index

Word Count: 194

Grade: 1

Early-Intervention Level: 22